The Song of North Mountain

Morgan Golladay

ISBN: 978-1-957224-25-1

Printed in the United States of America.

FIND US AT
oldscratchpress.com
currentwords.com

CONTENTS

DEDICATION

As a post-war child faced with increasing numbers of others my age and younger, overcrowding in schools was the norm, not the exception. Every teacher I had during the seven years before I entered high school taught a minimum of 32 students. We were a mixed group of studious and active kids, with all levels of an ability to grasp what we were being taught.

Looking back, I understand how our teachers struggled on an hourly basis, for they had to command science, literature, math, art, and too many other fields, and they taught us by themselves, relying only on their own educations, peers, books, and prayer.

This chapbook is dedicated to all of them, even those I did not like. For they gave me enough quiet time and freedom to do the things I love the best – to read. To explore. To discover words.

Thank you, all of you, for your struggles, your hopes, your kindnesses, and your love of learning.

MG

THE POET

I am a truth-teller.
I touch on things
your heart has forgotten,
your lips have not the words for,
your secrets buried deep in your soul,
your fears, lurking around corners,
your joys, too rich to be described.

I break through the veil of our parallel worlds,
our deepest desires,
our unanswered questions left unspoken.

I am versed in the subtleties
of language, emotion, memory,
and I give you minute opportunities
to see, to understand, to revel and cry
at the vast changes this life has to offer.

I tell you stories of myself,
and in them you find yourself.

ACKNOWLEDGMENTS

Thanks to the following books and periodicals, both online and print, in which these poems first appeared.

Broadkill Review, Old Tools, River Run

Halloween Party '21, Devil's Throne, The Gravid Doe

Instant Noodles, Starfire, River Road

Solstice, A Winter Anthology, v. 2, December Mist

Continuing thanks go to the members of the Milton Workshop for their thoughts and critique of many of the poems that appear here. Through their encouragement of me as an emerging poet, this book, and the courage to publish it, has been made possible.

The Song of North Mountain

Whether in sea or fire, in earth or air,

The extravagant and erring spirit hies

To his confine.

Wm. Shakespeare

Hamlet I, i, 153

Fire

Starfire

The star that fell to earth last night
was captured in this yellow puff,
this ground-hugging dandelion
barely lifting its head to the sun.
The free exchange, stardust
to starlife,
seeds itself in my mind,
a reminder of connection,
of creation, of the impossibility
of everything I believe.

That a star, burst from the night sky,
could become a pincushion of brightness
beneath my feet
must require the focus of magic,
both earth and sky,
to transform from starburst to starfire.

Dawn Veil

A single warbler's song
echoed through the long, thin cloud
that hung across Schoolhouse Mountain.
The veil turned slowly from rose,
to pink, to yellow, then quietly disappeared
as the sun warmed the treetops.
The rockslide changed from grey to blue
in the morning light.
Life stirred.
The curtain lifted.
I waited.

The foxes might come,
kits gamboling among the boulders.
Perhaps the bear
will lope through the briars,
snuffling for berries to plunder.

I wait, and the answers come
as slanting rays pierce the cloak
that enfolds Schoolhouse Mountain.

Morning Star

I love to watch the morning star
as she fades into the sunrise,
her brightness dimmed and overshadowed
by the greater sun.
Venus is regular in my sky,
and I wake to embrace her constancy,
her sign that all is well.

The silence of the dawn
breaks as the robins, wrens,
cardinals and redwings
sing their love songs to her.

I then go about my work
and rest, anticipating
new songs, new greetings, new beginnings
as the morning star
welcomes me the next new day.

Cricket Song

The heat of the day
erased all odor from the air,
except for a dry, dusty smell of dying.
The drought would be broken by storm,
but the runoff would leave no lasting benefit.
A far distant aquifer would swell,
subside, and pass on to the sea.
The river would rage momentarily,
then recede again into acquiescence.

Tonight I will sit on my porch,
hoping the swelter of the day will ease,
and the night-bloomers –
moon flowers, gardenias, nightshades –
might offer some relief to my senses.
Dusk will bring the birds to feed,
cardinals, finches, doves,
all in their turns.
Crickets will embrace the moisture under
the now-full birdbaths,
and sing to the stars.

Duskfall

Late evening light casts long shadows
across the grass.
My mountains turn gold,
briefly, ecstatically,
as they kiss the sun goodnight.
I raise my hand,
wishing them peaceful slumbers,
knowing they will not sleep,
but dream in the silence
of the stars.
Our shadows merge,
the ridges, trees, grasses, flowers,
and that of the dog.
For this short moment
we are one,
as night bids hello to the world,
and a different life begins.

River Road

The river road
strode unshod,
dustily to the ford.
August's heat
lay close to the ground.
Dust imps,
too tired to be full-fledged devils,
cast their wings aside
and rested in the grass.
Our rope-swing broke years ago,
so we sloshed to limpid pools,
longing for relief,
waiting for storm breaks,
promised, yet unfulfilled.

The river was low,
and the ford, clearly visible,
led us to the other side,
to earnest shade,
beneath wilting trees,
as we yearned for rain.

Under the Locusts

In the far corner of Vincent's pasture,
where the grown-over lane spread its unchecked growth
and reached out to encompass the field,
a group of seven locust trees stood,
the only shade, the only respite his cattle had
to escape August's hot sun.
When even their pond slowly dried up, the steers would still come,
seeking some small solace in the cool,
nibbling on encroaching honeysuckle, briars,
any thing to give moisture and sustenance
when summer pasture grew sere.

Long after the farm was abandoned,
the evidence of thousands of hoof-falls showed among the locusts.
Roots stood stark and barren, surrounding dirt worn and blown away.
Strange shapes, mystical and druidic in their formation,
reared from the dirt, submerging, reappearing several feet away.
Still a shady spot, even in winter,
if one listened carefully,
the faint echo of calls and hoofbeats could be heard.

I long for that hot pasture where the cattle grazed,
to be free from eyes that seek to ensnare me within their will,
free from any thought other than the glaring heat,
the dry prickles of grass beneath my legs
as I sit and remember.

Old Tools

When I loaded the tools
into the back of the car,
the shovels' polished handles
and sharpened blades,
the rakes, splayed with caught branches,
tines broken,
spading forks, long and short-handled,
(yours was the long one),
I did not grieve.

Even at the unloading,
the receiver would have no idea
of the cords of wood split and stacked.
These were simply tools, mauls, axes, wedges,
not symbols of someone's life.

I think about my grandfather, the blacksmith,
how, at the final sale and dispersal
by the executor and auctioneer,
no one there could fathom the finality of
the life, the skill, the personality
radiating from his tools.

Air

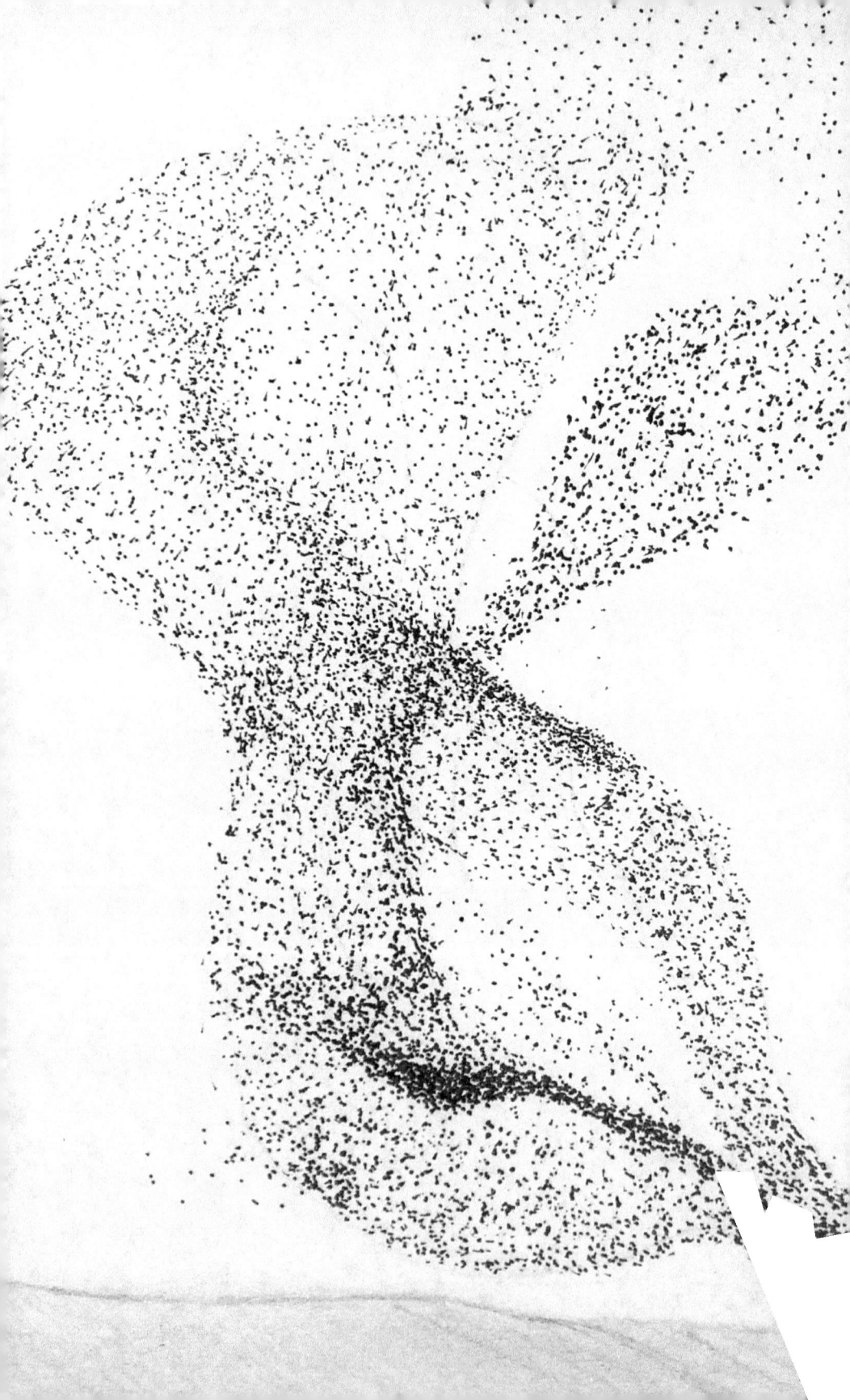

Morning Song

Sometimes,
in the quiet of the morning,
before the rest of the world stirs,
I hear the earth breathing.
Winds sigh,
branches rustle,
grasses and leaves quiver,
all with anticipation
of this new day,
unlike all others,
but
the same.

I dress quickly
and go to the pond,
the peepers and I sing our Good Mornings
to each other,
and we laugh with the sun.

Ghost Light

Looking back along the ridge
a thin rib of light briefly
illuminates the forest floor
and silhouettes trees stark against winter sky.
Look too soon
and you miss the mystery
of Dillon's Mountain's brief farewell
to nightsky and stars and sweet Venus.
Look too late
and the slumbering giant
lumbers slowly
into its ordinary dayspring.

But if you should,
by chance or intent,
catch the moment,
you will see life
and hope
renewed
in a sudden shaft of dawnbreak.

Mourning Dove

Downy fluff
floated to the grass,
joining its sisters
plucked before their time.
The dove, limp and bloodied,
hung crookedly across a branch,
secure in the talons of a red-tail.
His burning hunger abated,
the cleaving continued,
dissecting muscle from bone.
Leavings were left to the small ones,
the mice, voles, beetles who gleaned.
Grievings were left to her mate.
Mourning, now forever, the male became his name.

Winter Morning

The woods are smoldering
under the shifting weight of pre-dawn fog,
trapped in the coolness of the trees.
Mists have long since
burned off barren fields,
but fires of creation,
banked for a long night of winter,
rise smoke-like through the day.
I turn,
mindful of my steps,
my mind racing with the awareness of ideas.
Images tumble in this morning of creation,
and I reach for my pencil.

Just a Walk in the Woods

I left the car in my neighbors' yard,
near the old hay rake.
They knew my love of the mountain,
the ridge, the rockfall,
the fire tower overlooking the river.

The grass in the yard was dry,
sere in the September heat.
My jacket was in my small pack,
water, apples, bread, cheese.
I would be gone all day.

I cut across the meadow,
past the makeshift sluice that carried water
from the spring to the pond,
across the stone wall, and straight up the slope.
This grade was easy,
but I would need to tack as the land got steeper.
No need to risk a fall or a sprain.

Handholds were easy,
small saplings, stray branches, occasional rocks.
I made sure to make noise,
alerting the small ones I was coming
with my staff striking stone and root.
Even at this low elevation
I could see signs of drought stress
among the smaller trees and ferns.

A thousand feet, and I would be at the wagon trail,
The sky, the birds, the treetops.

These old trees, with deep roots
penetrating the mountain
would find the water they needed.
And above all else,
the green life of the woods would surround me,
there, where the trees touched the sky.

The Gravid Doe

She lay still.
Beautiful in her death,
the mourners gathered,
dressed in accustomed black,
waiting for the funeral feast.
Undeterred by passing traffic,
they blessed the bounty,
crowded to the altar,
dipped their beaks
and fed.

My thoughts return
to cycles.
There is a beauty and a rhythm
in this continuing story:
she feeds these vultures,
who, like me,
will eventually feed others.

Old Woman

I envision Spring as an old woman,
being helped up the mountain by
a younger self,
pausing often, dispersing new green
from her bag of wonder,
newness slowly coloring the slopes,
covering the bareness of the trees,
their branches harsh against the sky,
with life and leaf and flower.

Cicadas

It was past midnight,
the porch beckoned,
darkness fighting with the omniscient lights
surrounding our buildings.
The pastures across the road
comforted the cows,
content with their cuds
and grass and each other.
A few vague travelers on the road
left only the hum of tires echoing off our walls,
and a burst of light
pulling them to destinations unknown.
Momentary interruptions in a cooling night,
a few sparrows complaining, resettling,
cicadas quieting, sleep gripping the world.

Milky Way

Even with the huge bonfire
lighting our faces and friends,
we could still see the stars
covering the sky between the treetops.
Down in the meadow
on our nightwalk
to the river,
the Milky Way arced
across the August sky.
It was a cusp,
a turning point,
a last goodbye.
Little bark boats carried our wishes
far down the river,
to an eternity of memories.
We felt the sadness of the coming separation
as a weight that dragged us onward.
Our footsteps in the dusty track
left no sign of our passing.
But the echoes remain in our hearts,
resurfacing every time we see the Milky Way
split the night.

December Mist

There,
at the edge of Vincent's wood,
morning fog
is lifting off pastures
covered with winter stubble.
Sunlight reflects blue
off the banded mist,
begotten by yesterday's
warm sun on December earth.
The gods of soil and field
slumber still,
cold slowly settling into their bones.

I walk the verge, waiting, watching.
My duties are elective,
my life linear,
unlike the seasons.
I greet this Solstice
with calm, measured footsteps,
waiting and watching
as cycles turn.

In the Treetops

There is little air stirring
on the forest floor,
even in this small clearing.
The canopies of
mighty oaks and pillar pines
thrust and sway,
dancing to a wind
we can only see
by what it leaves behind –
slender branches
whipping in errant breezes.

Sunbeams and shadows are alive,
vying for territory on the forest undergrowth.
The high sun pierces the blanket of leaves
in small spaces, constantly moving
across the leaf litter, playing tag
with the shade.
When sunset draws near,
the air stills, the trees pause for breath as
branches and breeze end their dance.

Spring on the Mountainside

Spring,
malingering in the cold,
creeps cautiously
up North Mountain.
Hidden swales of frost
hold fast
to the quiet stillness of winter.

Out on the Devil's Throne
careful briars show green,
warming, like me, in the heat of the sun.
Redbuds languish,
eagerly waiting to erupt,
to be first, to show true color
to this mountain.
I trust in their uncompromising cycles,
that spring follows winter
as night follows day.
The redbuds beckon me up the mountain.

Fullness of Time

This morning I hastened to leave
the shelter and warmth of my home.
I headed to the mountain
which had beckoned me
through the long equinox eve.

The old wagon trace along the ridge
still held last week's snow,
trapped deep in the ruts.
The barely discernible memory
of ancient carts informed the young saplings
that this was not the place to grow,
and larger vehicles still used the track.

Today, Spring is crawling
at its own pace,
rushing headlong across the fields below,
lingering in a copse of redbud and dogwood,
gathering vision in the scent of warm sun.
A mood of greening and expectation of change
underlies the stillness.

There is no time on the mountain,
no tape measure, no division of hours,
only the sun moving across the sky
and the slow pace of clouds rolling down the slopes.
Snow lingers among the boulders,
mist ghosts through the trees,
Spring creeps up the slope.

Water

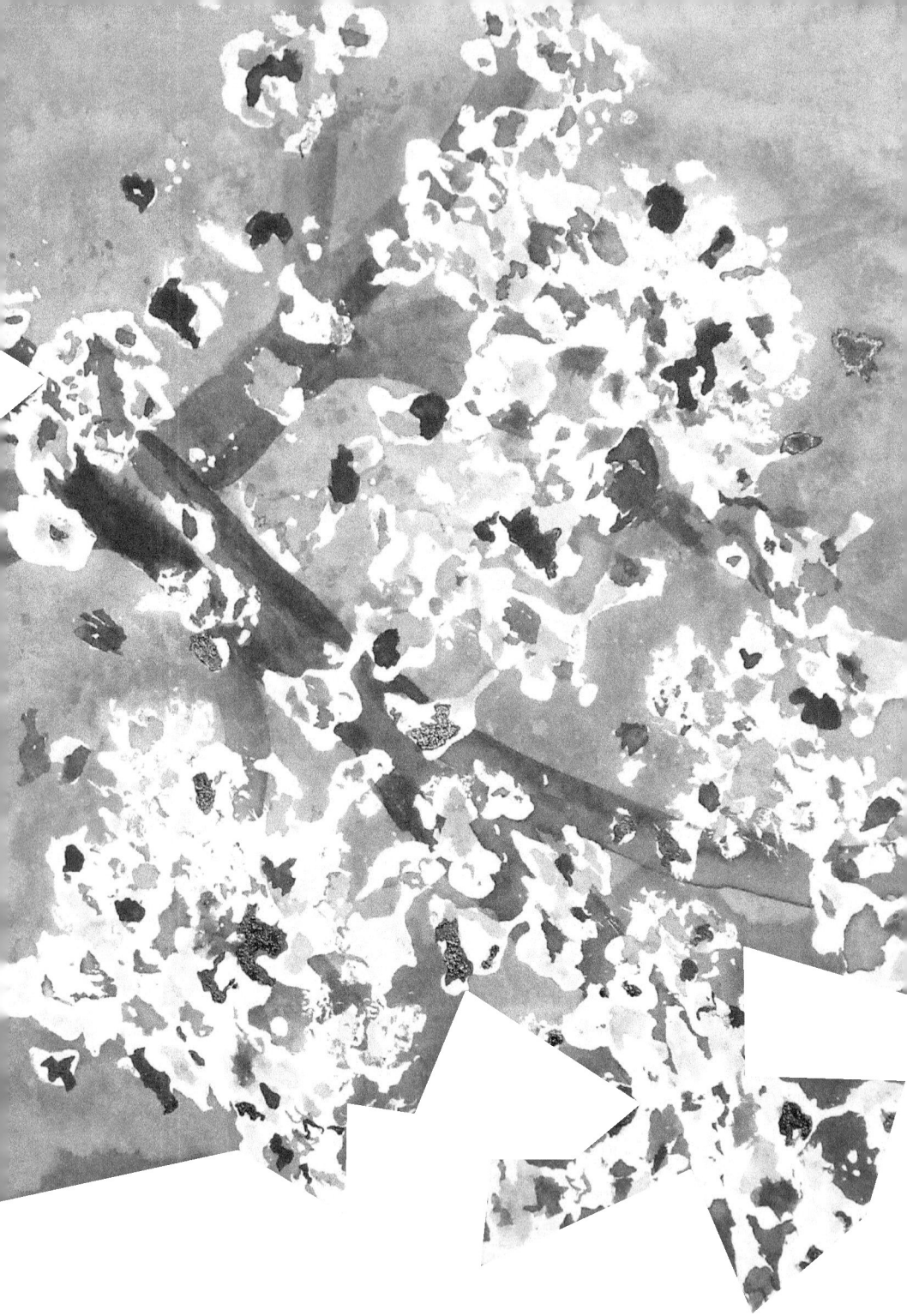

Unintended Gift

As I stood in the ditch
by Taylor's Pond,
dark mud oozing up my shins,
April chill filling my shoes,
I stumbled,
nearly fell
as the waking earth
grasped at me
with longing.

I left a gift,
not wishing to stay.
Duty, and fear, hastened me away,
But I gave
for some future wader
or archaeologist to find,
one yellow hi-top, circa 2019.

The Flow

Long days of rain made the ford impassable.
At the bend, a low field flooded,
dark, muddy water
smothering the spring grasses.
The water would leave layers of noxious silt
to be reclaimed by new grasses.

I sat on the high bank,
watching the rough water climb ten feet
to scour tree roots where I perched.
Tonight, the meadow behind me would flood,
drowning any small ones
who had not forsaken the safety of their burrows.
The road across the river was being undercut.
The river did not care;
it did as nature, and the rain, required.

Later,
I could trace with my feet the edge of high waters
by its rims of detritus.
Branches, caked mud, tangles of grass and leaves.
The meadow would restore this,
creating new life from the destructive anger of the river.

West of Marlboro

We watched summer storms build,
scudding across North Mountain.
Old weather eyes knew
that bad storms came up through the gap,
down west of Marlboro.
Too full to pass higher over the mountains,
they held clouds heavy with rain,
low thunder and wind.
Those were the ones that warned us,
bring in chickens and horses,
cover the beans, young cukes, succulents,
gather tools, cushions, chaises,
and bring in the laundry, whether wet or dry.
We would watch the rain track
across open fields, outbuildings, roads,
waiting for the sudden shock
of storm.

Low Water

The river crept over the ford,
threading its way between rocks
now risen above the water's reflection.
It had not rained for weeks.
Cattle called on dusty banks
that sloped to pools
left by the last flood's eddies.
It was a wide ford,
and shallow,
but we still could not walk it
without cool water
sloshing into our shoes.

What had been small torrents in June
had become August trickles and rock draughts,
small, barely consequential zephyrs of water
running more slowly to the sea.

The heat of the day
invited splashing,
and we reveled in our river-gifts,
low waters
softly flowing, gently soothing.

Along the Mountain Ridge

Along the mountain ridge
just off the old wagon road,
deep-rutted,
lined with rocks on either side,
I sit on my favorite log
and watch, but more, to listen.
The jays and crows compete for attention,
but no one heeds
until they screech of danger,
of intruder, of imbalance.

I wait, quiet, listening softly
to the mountain breathe and sigh.
The longing aches through ridges of granite and limestone,
softened by duff of ten thousand oaks, for ten thousand years,
but continuous, eternal.
The soft moans of a lover, heart-fast,
determined to return to the one who completes it,
to the valley, and the streams and swales below.
Little North Mountain wants for rain and wind
to speed its journey home.

Mixed Blessing

The cloud bank rolled down North Mountain
and settled at the edge of the Valley.
Heavy-laden with moisture,
it released a few snowflakes in the cold night air.
By morning, whiteness covered the farms and orchards,
hiding the roads and tracks.
More snow was promised
as the clouds, too burdened to move,
birthed a blizzard, aided by
a fierce northwest wind.

Quiet hung in the air when the wind abated.
Wood smoke from chimneys was indistinguishable from falling snow.

The roads drifted shut behind the snowplows,
unable to keep up with the wind the next week.
The Eskimo-Aleut language has hundreds of words for snow.
Most of the farmers, teachers, shop owners had only one – nuisance.
We children had a different one – no school.

We soon grew tired of reshoveling paths,
unbuildable snowmen, wet boots and mittens, and frosty fingers.
Adults were tired of the standstill, the forced isolation, no mail.
All were delighted when life returned to normal.

Come spring, lost school days were made up
on Saturdays and reclaimed holidays.
The warm May days, with the smell of new-mown grass
drifting through the open school bus windows,
made us realize, snow is a mixed blessing.

At Taylor's Pond

The little heron stealthily circles the pond,
wading slowly in the shallows,
there, where the water undercuts the bank.
He is about his business – fishing.
I am about mine – watching.
I come here regularly,
to observe his quiet habit,
his flash, his keen eye.
There is a lesson of patience,
of determination, of concentration.
I come away
slowly through the grasses
and across the lane,
remembering the unspoken lecture,
to pay attention
to the now,
to the present moment.

The Channel

We placed the stones together tightly,
creating a trough,
a niche
where the water would flow
across the last uneven patch,
channeled now to the pool
from the spring on the mountainside.
It was our thought to ease the path
the water took over rubble
and hard scrabble,
arriving clearer and cleaner,
without debris or leaf mold.

The next day
we removed the stone gutter.
Litter clogged its channel;
the water had detoured,
creating a new path.
This new obstacle we had created
was well-intended.
But in the end,
we removed the barrier
and let the stream find its own course.

On My Back

I lie on my back in the grass
by Taylor's Pond.
Newly mown, the verge is sweet,
crickets singing.
An occasional fish,
a sunnie, I think, breaks the surface
with a tinkling plop.
My eyes are on the sky,
watching clouds amble without direction
across an azure skyground.
All I can see is infinity.
Beyond that is the Milky Way,
the unknowing,
and eventually,
the face of god.

River Run

I stand in the ford,
gravel quiet beneath my feet,
water surging around my shins.
Over the centuries
the river run has worn the rocks
smooth, removing imperfections,
softening edges, creating forms.
Just behind the larger boulders,
the water turns milky, then clear,
losing its pearlescence as it returns to itself.
Afternoon light sparkles brightly
as waters surge and ripple.
I cup my hands into this coursing source of life.
Even in my hollowed palms,
this brew of oxygen and hydrogen
retains its form,
languid, fluid, gleaming in the sun.
When I return this water to its source,
I cannot tell which was in my hands,
which was not.

August Rain

A small clap of thunder
sends the cat scurrying.
Light, steady rain follows.
Traffic noise increases
this early morning.
Tires greeting wet pavement
are satisfying sounds
as I sit and close my eyes to
the distraction of phones ringing, doors shutting.
Busyness continues without me.

My mind drifts to yesterday's walk,
ambling across the sunny fields to the pond.
I imagine the sunnies leaping
above the surface, flying through a different pond –
the air of their new home in the rain.
The little egrets have no need
of boots or rain slickers.

I remember reveling in rain,
lying on the grass in rain,
bathing in rain.
And while my youthful energy
has vanished like those rains
and soaked into the experiences of yesterday,
the memories remain
as fresh as this August rain on the grass.

Under Schoolhouse Mountain

Across the great meadow,
ochre and sere in the summer heat,
we trudge at forest verge
to the dock.
Our canoes rest
high on the bank
and are heavy with canvas,
aged with layers of paint.
We will practice swamping
and righting
and entering from the water
over gunwales polished
by many attempts to reboard.

At half flood-height,
the river is shallow enough to stand in.
We could cheat,
and slip to the ford,
but we seek the deeper channel –
to prove we are able,
to prove we are strong,
to prove we are indeed
both mermaids and children of the forest.

Floating on the River

We would lie back
on the surface,
letting sweet summer water carry us,
carry us, carry us
as cruciform beings,
floating bark boats.
Laughing, bumping into shallows,
dragging heels and pockets
across pebbles worn to smoothness,
featureless from the movement and flow,
we focused on sky,
treetops,
and the changing changelessness
of skimming, being, emerging ourselves
into oneness with the river.

Mooring

The day after our dock broke loose
we trudged the river,
finding it snagged on a broken limb far downstream.
The dock itself was not of value,
except as labor and creativity
to imagine and build it.
But it was ours,
well-used, well-loved, well-cared for,
drums and canvas replaced each year.
It was a jumping-off point
for swimmers and canoes.
The river had returned to normal,
easily waded, cleanly swum.
We tied ropes to hook the dock
and hauled it the thousand yards
against the current
back to its berth.
Our labor invested the river with supernatural power
and blessed exposed tree roots with our song.
We toiled the dock home,
where, we, too, were safely moored.

Porter's Pond

Their pond was vast, huge.
So large, I could not see where
the water met the shore on the far side.
Our ponds were small, but large enough
for cattle to drink.
Porous limestone and shale channeled excess rain
quickly into underground streams and aquifers.
This one was different.
Mountain-rimmed, treescaped,
a place for ducks, geese, turtles, muskrats,
deer to drink and play.
I was rooted,
amazed at the immensity,
awed at the possibility,
inundated with the idea of swimming,
really swimming.
The closest thing I knew was the quarry,
filled with water from an underground river,
icy cold, and forbidden to us.

But this pond –
this pond –
this pond
was alive with the magic
of tantalizing possibility.

Water Skippers

Ten thousand drops of rain
pierced the surface of the pond,
followed by ten thousand more.
A few venturous water striders,
the surface tension allowing their long legs
to skip across the dark pool,
watched as skies emptied.
Most had sought harbor
at pond's edge.
I, too, sought refuge
under overhanging pines,
waiting for the dance to continue.

The skippers only touch the surface
as they skate across the open water.
Quiet depths, waiting and reaching,
invite us to risk, to come deeper
and explore transformation.

We waited to meet ourselves
while ten thousand drops of water fell.

Little Swimmer

The cottonmouth swam to us,
curving serpentine ripples in its wake,
just its head surging above the surface.
I was surprised,
not knowing they could swim,
and fearful of it hitching a ride.
It paced us for several yards,
then veered to the opposite bank,
preferring the cool of the duff
to July heat in an aluminum canoe
coasting downriver.
We paddled on,
and never spoke of the snake,
its sinuousness, its sensuality,
its gathering danger,
the wonder of it sharing its world with us.

Earth

The Shed Antler

The antler wobbled, fell,
shed in the brambles at the base of a tree.
The nearby spring
welcomed the buck,
who would soon lose the other antler
to the annual cycle.

Hours later,
I walked through the April wood,
looking for signs of life,
new growth, a bit of joy
pried from a cold, wet March.
The antler gleamed softly
in the late afternoon light.
Water gurgled softly nearby,
hoofprints still wet in the mud.
The honeysuckle held the shed
to the sky.

I, in my frailty,
would surely hesitate
when it was time to discard my protection,
yielding it up so gracefully
to go forth into the world,
vulnerable
and anticipating change.

Valley Hills

On this slope
the ridges of stone
slowly erode,
warmed by a thousand, thousand suns,
chilled by the snows of eternity,
quiet in their world.
They have seen massive storms,
sunrises beyond the magnitude of imagination,
fire, flood, survival,
breathing slowly,
exhaling over a century,
watching, being, always present.

These limestone ridges worn by water and wind,
smoothed by grazing lips of cattle,
deer, mice, and rabbits,
are too scrabbled to plow,
breaking the shares into unforgiveable pieces.
In shallow swales between outcrops,
orchardists tend their trees,
the land fit only for fruit, or scrub pine,
or livestock.

The skeleton and bones of the Valley,
its bedrock pillows, sheets, exposures,
will endure past herds, wildlife,
even the orchard grasses,
while the land slumbers and rests.

Family Lines

The lots are overgrown with weeds, brambles,
saplings jutting through loose stones
that mark lost foundations.
Someone once lived here.
Someone planted those surviving daffodils,
that stray lilac.

Sunday dinners, visitations, funerals,
jam-making, weddings, and scrubbed floors
celebrated the families that lived here.
(Their footprints are found
when the yard is tidier.)
But the rubble remembers the sweat and the labor,
the daffodils recall the hands that planted them.

Over the years the family dispersed,
separated by war, disaster,
marriage, changes in fortune.
The children married into other families,
staying, leaving,
moving farther away from their first home.

The overgrowth and understory
becomes a new foundation,
calling me back to the sheer awe of
seeing the work of their hands,
and sharing the same space.
Although I do not know their faces or names,
I wonder at the stories they could tell.

Hedge Row

There, at the end of Bradford's dry-stone wall,
brambles had overtaken the wooden rails,
gradually pulling them apart.
The split logs were returning to mounds of dust,
rotted past recognition and use.
Hidden deep beneath unkempt banks
of wild grapevine and honeysuckle
was a thigh bone –
a steer gone missing
decades ago,
now as unrecognizable as the fence.

This is how my future will overtake me -
at the edge of the lane,
covered by creepers
that outlasts time.
Those eternal vines reduce
and change and create
newness from dirt and decay,
freshening life from loss.
I want to return as a wild rose,
or with luck, as sweet honeysuckle.

Back in the Woods

The great boulder, large as a room,
lay buried in feet of thick duff
laid down by thousands of years of oaks and pines,
breathing and living across their age.
A massive crack ran its length,
wide enough for me to pass through.
Sundered, this rock would never be whole.

I lay on its top, listening to the breeze stir leaves.
Quiet rustles in the leaf fall invited me
to wait, to wonder, to explore a different life
that connected me to a breathing earth.

Within the circle of my vision
this universe was vast, endless,
and I was brief,
only a small whisper in its existence.
But, for all my short span in this world,
I experienced the magic and awe of
a creation larger than I could imagine.

"Rest with us," whispered the granite.
"Breathe with us," crooned the breeze.
"Stay with us," encouraged the trees.

Climbing

I no longer climb trees.
But, it is not the fault of the trees.
Thick limbs,
foot braces and handholds
are still reliable,
still willing, still steadfast.
No, if fault is to be assigned,
it is mine.
The insecurity of age
limits my confidence,
unsure of my strength,
my balance.

Ah, but the anticipation
of firemen rescuing me
from a tall, forked oak,
like an overconfident cat,
does have its temptations.

A Moment of Grace

The rustle of dry leaves caught me, there at the roadside.
The gravel track was weed-grown, but the enticing crinkle
came from the short thicket at the edge.
A chipmunk, I thought, or a mouse.
Quick, elusive, I'd be lucky to see it.
Kneeling, patient, slowly separating
winding briars and grasses, it was there,
brown and golden and dappled
in bursts of sunlight through overhanging leaves.

Slowly, cautiously, the box turtle raised his head,
sniffed, and picked a raspberry from a dangling stem.
Juice streamed freely from his horny mouth.
He did not smile, but his eyes glowed with delight.

His world was small, his life travels
would not exceed a mile from his birthplace.
But all he needed in this moment
was a sweet treat and juice staining his chin.
We spoke in silence,
thanking each other for dappled sunlight, ripe berries,
and a moment of grace.

The Song of North Mountain

I

Behind our neighbor's farmhouse,
the pasture creeps up the mountain.
Cattle grazing on ripe grass
avoid the hollow, sensing danger.
The mountain, however,
continues its slumber,
stretching quietly,
folding, embracing the trees and saplings
blanketing its slopes.
Undergrowth, May apples,
wild violets, ferns and mosses
vie for shade and moisture,
all seeking to spread their roots.
Mountain laurel reaches to the sun,
unworried, grateful for light,
for rain, for the balance
of give and take.

II

There was a rustle in the leaves
as the doe stepped out.
She watched.
Two fawns tiptoed beside her.
Her head raised, she sniffed,
and took another step.

III

These ridges are fraught with fissures,
some only rockfall shelters
habited by bears and cats
until they were killed off.
The bigger caves are empty now,
except for mountain-fed streams and rainfall
that erodes the soft limestone,
entrances hidden by vegetation,
slipped, slow landslides,
and intentional walls.
They allow the mountain to breathe.

Within the mountain is a marvel,
a chasm with cold air escaping,
and ice forming within.
Further down the chain,
larger caverns have been cleared of mud,
tinted red from oxides leached from the soils above.
Tourists come to see these wonders
of creation made visible,
but not made by man.
What should the angels say
were they to walk in these halls of wonder?
Would they, too, be in awe?

IV

Big North Mountain rests.
Snow-shrouded crest
undulates under a storm sky.
The birds seek shelter below,
in thicket and underbrush.
The mountain is impartial,

having its own priorities,
its own needs,
its own necessity.
Even this mountain,
created before time,
is changing, eroding, returning to the Valley.
With eternities of moments,
the snows, freezes and thaws,
unseasonal rains,
even the life on its slopes,
will change its form,
soften its faces,
gentle its heights as it sinks into itself.

V

The song of the mountain
comes whispering down its slope.
As mist gathers in vales and hollows,
so the mountain's deep, slow thrumming
coalesces in the empty spaces of my heart.
My soul-fire, long banked, sparks;
embers catch with new air,
nurturing a burning desire
to create, to risk, to explore,
to strike out and return,
and then to sink into the desires
this quiet witness nourishes.

The Broken Point

I kicked a clod in the cornfield
below Schoolhouse Mountain,
down by the river bend.
Flooding had long passed,
and water was low.
Heavy and dry,
the lump fell apart at my feet.

It lay there, encrusted with clay
and small gravel,
a spear point,
lost or abandoned, edges still sharp,
the tip broken.
Web and shaft
had returned to dust and decay
centuries, centuries ago.
No bigger than the palm of my hand,
it could have slain bear, elk, buffalo,
or man.

This place is mine on loan.
Many others lived here before,
many others will after.

I took a coin out of my pocket
and pressed it deep into a furrow,
next to the broken point.

Silas

Cornstalks stand bent and broken
in the snow-crusted field.
The February sun,
just brightening the nearby treetops,
will eventually reveal
the ruined crops, black and withered.
The single-minded cold raises ghost-fog
off furrows long neglected.

I know his story,
his battles against weather,
grief, the bank, personal demons,
a risk taken and unfulfilled.

He moved back to town in the fall.
I met him in the grocery,
clerking for some nameless corporation,
barely remembering his dreams
of sky, sun, warm earth cupped in his hands.

We all lose our dreams,
some quickly, like a knife-thrust,
others more slowly, by teaspoons and forgotten sunsets.
But all eventually erode into the dust
of faded memory.

Pine Field

Down below the house
in five extra acres my dad bought
when he built our new home,
we planted pine trees
in orderly rows and progressions,
hauling water, tamping soil,
clearing grasses,
waiting.
Waiting for the field mice to make their runs,
and the foxes to chase the rabbits,
waiting for the trees to grow above the weed-tops.
Tall, whistling gracefully in the breeze,
they were my friends, my sanctuary,
the safety of my childhood.
We grew tall together.

The property my brother inherited
has been sold.
My friends are gone now,
harvested. Cruelly cut.
Did no one thank or praise them?
Or greet them?
I always thought they belonged to themselves, not to us.

Where, now, will the butterflies rest
in their migration,
now the trees are gone?

White Parasols

Queen Anne's Lace
stand daintily in their habit,
wild in their expressions of joy.
They grow in the waste land,
marking the border
between wood and lane.

A multitude of flowerets
form the canopy,
defined by space and air
between them,
like their namesake lace.

Small tumbleweeds of seeds,
held together by dried stems
of spent flowers,
share the wealth of
sudden grace in August verges.

Train Whistle

The tracks were always shiny,
and we would occasionally
place pennies on the near side
to retrieve later as flattened souvenirs,
oval keepsakes for our pockets.
We couldn't tell Mr. Lincoln's face
from the wheat sheaves.

The trains diminished in length
and frequency over long years,
but the 9pm freight train
lulled me to sleep
with its at-crossing whistle.

Even now, sixty years on,
a train shrieking in the night
evokes a time of gravel lanes,
still nights and occasional cricket serenades,
windows wide to occasional summer breezes,
and sitting asleep in the back seat of the car,
the vinyl sticking to my sweaty legs.

The Old Man

I could imagine the Old Man in the Mountain,
restless, preparing to waken,
or just rolling over to sleep another century,
pulling the quilt of the trees up over his shoulders.

Blanketed in upon itself,
the Massanutten stood out,
rick-rack crest dark against the bright sky.
I could see it, hear it call,
from my perch ten feet up the old maple
in the back yard.

The hogbacks appeared sewn together that afternoon,
dark shadows, darker than night,
accentuating the folds and patterns of the trees,
ridges leading to the valley.

The sun shifted slowly,
encompassing the gaps
in unconditional shadow.
I climbed down,
having witnessed the interwoven threads
of time and the mountain.

The Tree

We used to go out with our saws, hatchets,
ropes and buckets, bundled and booted in mid-December.
There were only a few cedars, strays, seeds dropped by passing birds
as they roosted in our pines.
Local orchardists rooted out and burned what cedars they found,
fearful of rust destroying their apples.
Ours were prized, saved and harvested for special.

Formerly rough pasture, the pine field sheltered quail and foxes,
hidden under rabbit brambles.
But we wanted a cedar tree,
and fragrant branches of white pine for the mantle and doors.
This hunting ritual was quiet,
apprising each for size, shape, would it be tall enough.
There was never sun spying on us, and seldom snow.
I would speak quietly to the trees,
fearful of question and taunting,
but still respectful of the life we took.

Eventually we grew and left the home place,
and a new tree became boxed and stored.
But we kept the last ritual of tying up pine boughs,
for nothing more than to welcome us home
to the warmth of family.

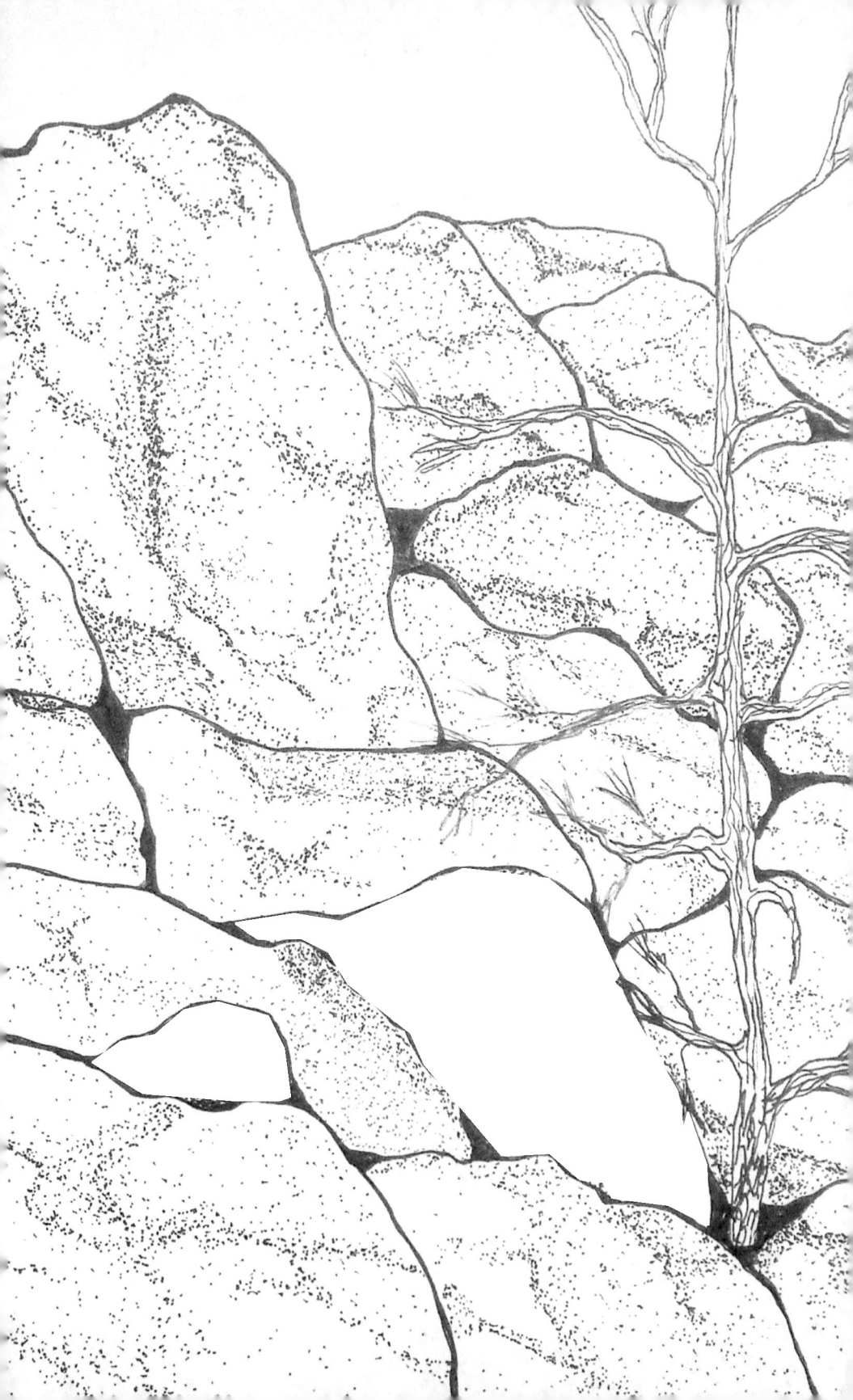

Devil's Throne

Across the Shenandoah,
over foothills at mountain's base,
you can catch a brief glimpse of the rockfall.
Centuries after the land slipped
on this, my mountain,
rains and winds moved the dirt,
subtly shifting soils and organics,
washing slides and rock faces clean.

All a-tumble,
these mountain bones are bare to the sun,
sheltering only a few hardy brambles
left by passing birds
and a slow-moving tide of stunted trees.
Locals call it Devil's Throne,
for he sat there, contemplating his fall,
and burning all life with his body's fire.

I think of it as a place of solitude,
strength, and sorrow,
home to small ones,
snakes, voles, mice;
a place of absolutes –
predator and prey.

Solitude

A murmuration danced
over the harvested wheat,
rising and twisting,
flowing as a huge beast of the air.

I sat quietly
as small ones
followed their patterns
around me.

White-tipped fox tails
bounced on the rocks,
confident in the Devil's
eternal absence from his throne.

They carried nothing with them,
the foxes or the starlings,
only their joy in sunshine
and air.

About the Author

The Song of North Mountain is a love song to the hills, rivers, and ridges of the Shenandoah Valley of Virginia, but most particularly to Great North Mountain. Morgan Golladay grew up between the Blue Ridge and North Mountain, and the daily changes in the visual presence of the mountains and land have influenced the work in this chapbook. She has drawn upon her memories and experiences in conjuring images and thoughts of living in this rural valley where the sky kisses the mountaintops and the rain moves through the gaps.

As you can read in the dedication, Golladay's grade schoolteachers had a great influence on her writing. All of their insistence on vocabulary, syntax, and structure provided a springboard for her detailed imagery in the concise, simple, and tight lines that appear in this book.

Although she has only shared her work in publication since 2020, Golladay has been thrice recognized by the Delaware Press Association (DPA) for her poetry. More recently, her short story, "Under the Rhododendrons," published in *Halloween Party '23* (Gravelight Press) placed first in the short story category in the DPA's 2024 Communication Contest Awards. Another of her short stories, "Second Christmas," published in the 2023 anthology *Solstice: Volume 3* (Devil's Party), placed second in the aforementioned competition. *The Song of North Mountain* is her first book of poetry.

A graduate of the University of Mary Washington, her watercolors and acrylic-collage paintings have won multiple awards. She has published other short stories and is currently editing her first novel and working on two more. She lives in Milford, Delaware.

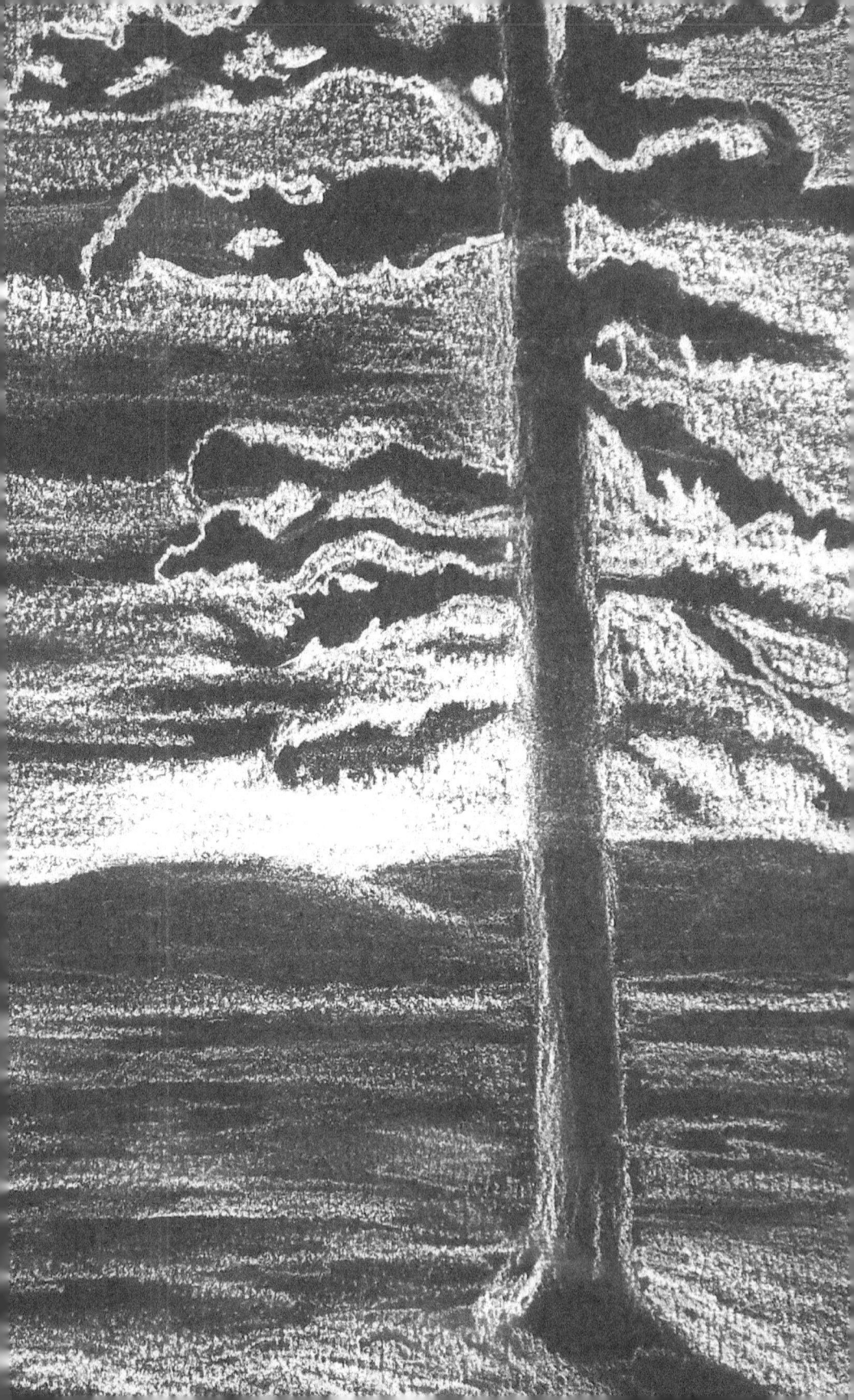

www.ingramcontent.com/pod-product-compliance
Lightning Source LLC
Chambersburg PA
CBHW071114120626
46546CB00003B/1335